# The Magic School Bus®
## PRESENTS
## Dinosaurs

**Scholastic Inc.**

Photos ©: 123RF: 3 bottom, 26 top left (Michael Heywood), 12 top left, 19 center left, 24 top left, 29 top left (Michael Rosskothen), 4 top left (Sergio Barrios); Alamy Images: 28 bottom left (Leonello Calvetti), 14 –15 (MasPix), 29 bottom left (Nobumichi Tamura/Stocktrek Images), 17 center left (Sabena Jane Blackbird); Dreamstime/Elena Duvernay: 20 –21, 26 –27; Getty Images: 6 –7 (Corey Ford/Stocktrek Images), 23 (Daniel Eskridge/Stocktrek Images), 24 right (Dorling Kindersley), 10 –11, 10 top left (Mark Stevenson/Stocktrek Images), 30 (Patrick Aventurier/Gamma-Rapho), 31 right (Ralph Lee Hopkins/National Geographic Creative), 20 top left (Sergey Krasovskiy/Stocktrek Images); iStockphoto: 14 top left (Elena Asenova), 29 top right (MR1805); National Geographic Creative/Mick Ellison: 16; Nature Picture Library/Juan Carlos Munoz: 4 –5; Science Source: 28 bottom right (Christian Darkin), 9 bottom left (Joe Tucciarone), 31 left (Pascal Goetgheluck), 22 bottom right (Phil Degginger/Carnegie Museum), 6 top left (Philippe Psaila), 12 bottom right (Richard T. Nowitz), 3 top, 3 center, 8, 13, 18, 29 bottom right (Roger Harris), 17 bottom right (Sinclair Stammers), 14 bottom left (Ted Kinsman); Shutterstock, Inc.: cover (Linda Bucklin), 9 top right (Michael Rosskothen); Superstock, Inc./Stocktrek Images: 22 top left; Thinkstock: 25, 28 top left (Elenarts), 1 (Linda Bucklin), 19 bottom right , 28 top right (MR1805).

ISBN 978-0-545-68583-2

Produced by Potomac Global Media, LLC

All text, illustrations, and compilation © 2014 Scholastic Inc.
Based on The Magic School Bus series © Joanna Cole and Bruce Degen
Text by Tom Jackson  Illustrations by Carolyn Bracken
Consultants: Rainer Newberry, Geology Professor, University of Alaska, Dr. Douglas Palmer, and Dr. Peter Rinkleff

Published by Scholastic Inc., 557 Broadway, New York, NY 10012.

12 11 10 9 8 7 6 5 4 3 2                                                                                   15 16 17 18 19/0

Cover design by Paul Banks
Interior design by Carol Farrar Norton
Photo research by Sharon Southren

Printed in the U.S.A.     40
First printing, January 2015

# Contents

p. 8

p. 18

p. 26

# Dinosaur Fossils

These footprints were left by a dinosaur walking through mud.

**W**ho likes museums?" asked Ms. Frizzle. Before anyone could answer, we found ourselves facing a huge skeleton with bones as thick as tree trunks! "That's a dinosaur fossil," said the Friz. "To see the real thing, hop on the bus and let's travel back in time!"

Many different kinds of dinosaurs lived on Earth. Scientists study their fossils to find out what they were like.

DIG IT!

**Ancient history!**

### When did dinosaurs live?
by Wanda

Dinosaurs died out about 66 million years ago (mya). Before that, they lived on Earth for about 165 million years. We know that dinosaurs changed a lot during that time because fossils found in older rocks are different from those found in newer rocks.

Triassic — Jurassic — Cretaceous

252 mya    201 mya    145 mya    66 mya

**Bones of stone**
Fossils are the remains of long-dead animals and plants that have turned into stone.

**Frizzle Fact**

The oldest dinosaur fossil ever found is about 240 million years old. It is from a Nyasasaurus, and it was found in Tanzania, Africa.

# Giant Animals

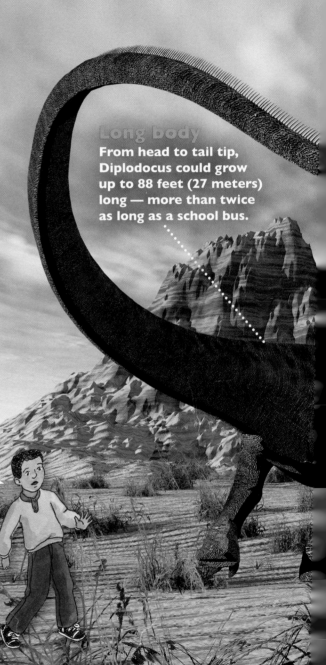

**D**inosaurs were the largest animals ever to walk the Earth. The biggest of them all belonged to a group of giant plant-eaters called sauropods. Fossils suggest that these animals could grow to 130 feet (40 meters) long and weigh as much as 14 elephants!

The largest dinosaurs ate leaves from huge ferns that grew as big as today's trees.

**Long body**
From head to tail tip, Diplodocus could grow up to 88 feet (27 meters) long — more than twice as long as a school bus.

This is a Diplodocus. Despite its size, it lived in herds to stay safe from predators.

**Frizzle Fact**
Eating plants all day wore down a dinosaur's teeth. A Diplodocus might grow a new tooth every 35 days.

**Hard facts!**

**Heads up**
This dino's head was small and light so Diplodocus could lift it up high.

## How did dinosaurs become fossils?
by Carlos

To become fossilized, an animal must be buried soon after it dies. Many of the dinosaurs we have fossils for drowned in mud or were buried in rock falls. The soft parts of the body, such as the skin, rotted away, but the harder bones and teeth stayed buried for millions of years. The sand or mud around the bones turned to solid rock. Water trickling through the rocks washed away the bones, leaving minerals in their place. Eventually, a bone-shaped stone was formed—a fossil!

# Mighty Hunters

**Frizzle Fact**

Scientists think that meat-eating Ornithomimus could run as fast as 40 miles (64 kilometers) per hour, making it the fastest two-legged animal ever to live on Earth.

T. rex would have been too heavy to run for long. It probably hunted by rushing out of the undergrowth and grabbing prey in its big jaws.

**D**inosaur predators had to be big, strong, or fast in order to catch and kill their giant prey. The most famous hunting dinosaur is Tyrannosaurus rex. Scientists think that T. rex walked on two legs and kept its balance using its long, strong tail.

Velociraptor had one long, sharp claw on each foot. It likely used the claw to tackle prey.

**Warming up**

Spinosaurus may have used its sail-shaped fin to catch the Sun's hot rays and warm up its blood.

# Mighty Spinosaurus

**An open-and-shut case!**

**Many teeth**

A long jaw full of teeth suggests Spinosaurus caught large fish or other animals that lived in water.

**Largest predator**

Spinosaurus was the largest hunting dinosaur.

## How hard could T. rex bite?

by Dorothy Ann

Scientists believe Tyrannosaurus rex had the strongest bite of any animal that has ever lived. They think it may have bitten three times as hard as the biggest sharks alive today.

The animal with the strongest bite today is the hyena—a scavenging animal that eats meat from bodies. It uses its strong jaws to crack through bones. Dinosaur experts think that T. rex ate by scavenging as well as hunting.

# Many Horns

Horns could be useful for fighting. Today, horned animals battle one another for top position in their herd. Perhaps dinos did, too.

**P**lant-eating Triceratops had long horns on its head and an armored shield of bone over its neck. This may have offered protection against attacks from large, predatory dinosaurs, which are thought to have killed their prey with a powerful bite to the head or neck.

Triceratops would stand and fight if a predator attacked.

I'd rather just run away!

**Chomp, chomp!**

## What did Triceratops eat?
by Keesha

Triceratops was a plant-eater, but it had no front teeth! Instead, fossils reveal a sharp beak made from bone. Experts say the dinosaur used this beak to grab leaves and twigs and to cut through them in the same way scissors cut paper.

Triceratops did have back teeth, and its jaw was more flexible than those of other dinosaurs. This means that Triceratops could chew its tough plant food before swallowing it.

Long horns were powerful weapons. They suggest heavy Triceratops would charge at an attacker and try to hurt it, just as a rhinoceros would do today.

# Armored Monsters

With such huge predators on the prowl, dinosaurs had different ways of protecting themselves. Some dinosaurs were small enough to run away and hide, while the bigger ones were covered in armor.

Stegosaurus had two rows of bony plates down its back and spikes on its tail, which it swung at predators.

Pachycephalosaurus had a domed skull made of thick bone. The dinosaur might have used it to butt heads with rivals or predators.

Pachycephalosaurus's thick skull was like a crash helmet.

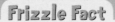

**Frizzle Fact**

Stegosaurus's plates may have been used as solar panels, soaking up the Sun's heat to warm the animal's blood.

Ankylosaurus was protected by bony spikes on its back. It also had a heavy lump of bone at the end of its tail, which it probably used as a club.

Piecing it together!

## How do we know what dinosaurs looked like?
by Phoebe

Scientists have discovered about 1,000 types of dinosaurs. But it is rare to find a complete fossil skeleton. For most species, all we have are a few bones. Experts can tell where in the body the bones would fit. Then they compare how the bones are shaped with bones of living birds and animals, to help figure out what a whole dinosaur looked like. Fossil teeth, jawbones, and claws are very useful clues. They tell the scientist how a dinosaur might have eaten.

# Duckbilled Dinosaurs

Hadrosaurs are known as duckbilled dinosaurs, because they had wide beaks that made them look like ducks. They were plant-eaters, and probably ate plants like pinecones and waterweed. They drank water, too. Some hadrosaurs had long crests on their heads.

Hadrosaurs had tough teeth that could crush up pinecones for eating.

Ew!

Fossilized droppings show what foods dinosaurs ate.

**Eating habits**

Hadrosaurs could stand tall on their back legs. Scientists think they also leaned forward on all fours to graze.

# Baby Dinosaurs

A mother watches her babies hatch. Newborn sauropods would have been easy targets for hungry predators.

**D**inosaurs hatched from eggs, just like birds and many reptiles do today. Experts say some dinosaurs buried their eggs in soil and leaves, while others laid them in nests on the ground. Some—but not all—dinosaurs guarded their eggs.

Eggheads!

How big were dinosaur eggs?
by Dorothy Ann

Dinosaur eggs varied in size. Some were much bigger than the birds' eggs you see today. For example, the eggs of large sauropods could be 2 feet (60 centimeters) wide. Dinosaur eggs had the same kind of shell as today's birds, and some were similar in shape, too. Others were round.

Giant Oviraptor egg

Chicken egg

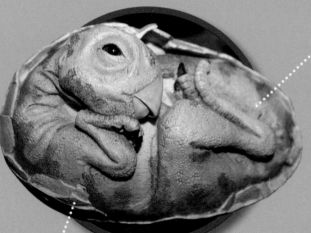

**Fossilized baby**
This baby dinosaur's bones were fossilized inside its egg after its nest was buried in sand.

**Thin shell**
The shell of a dinosaur egg was made of the same hard, chalky mineral as the shell of a bird.

Some dinosaur parents fed their young until they could look after themselves.

This hadrosaur nest is filled with round eggs. Like birds, dinosaurs built nests in warm, dry places.

# Water Reptiles

**Long neck**
A plesiosaur's flexible neck may have been too heavy for the reptile to hold up on land, but could have been useful for catching fish when it was in water.

**D**uring the dinosaur age, the oceans were filled with giant reptiles. The largest ones were 50 feet (15 meters) long. Scientists believe these water reptiles came to the surface to breathe air, just like today's whales and dolphins do. They didn't have legs, but instead had long, flexible flippers.

**Making waves!**

### All about ancient reptiles
by Ralphie

All dinosaurs were reptiles, but not all reptiles that lived in the time of dinosaurs were dinosaurs! For example, ocean reptiles are often referred to as dinosaurs, but actually belonged to a range of other types of reptiles. True dinosaurs were mainly land creatures, although a few lived in shallow water and there were even some that could fly.

### Shark eater
This huge jaw filled with teeth a bit like a crocodile's suggests that pliosaurs probably hunted for sharks.

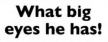

**What big eyes he has!**

This looks like a fish or a dolphin, but it was actually a reptile called an ichthyosaur. Experts say the reptile dived deep into the water to catch fish.

# High Fliers

It's possible that a pterosaur was able to fold up its wings and walk on all fours.

**T**he ancient skies were filled with flying reptiles called pterosaurs. Experts think that some launched themselves from trees and cliffs, while others took off from the ground. They flapped their wings and could soar like today's birds. Pterosaurs probably ate dead animals or scooped fish from the sea.

Keep up!

### Frizzle Fact

The pterosaur Quetzalcoatlus had a wingspan measuring 36 feet (11 meters) across. That almost matches the wingspan of the Wright brothers' plane.

**Firm grip**
Claws at the front of the wings probably helped with climbing.

Flap happy!

## All about pterosaur wings
by Tim

The first type of pterosaur discovered was named the pterodactyl, which means "wing finger." It got this name because fossils showed that the front edge of a pterosaur's long wing was actually a huge "finger" sticking out of the animal's front foot. The wing itself was a flap of skin that stretched from the "finger" to the top of the back legs.

**Comparing wingspans**

Albatross

Pterosaur

# Feathered Relatives

**W**hen people say dinosaurs have all died out, they are not exactly correct. You may have even eaten a dinosaur last Thanksgiving! That's because today's birds (including turkeys) are really a type of dinosaur that never died out. Birds probably evolved from small, tree-climbing dinosaurs that lived 150 mya.

Fossils suggest feathered Microraptor was closely related to birds. It had four wings and a long tail.

Experts think dinosaurs had feathers long before they had wings.

It's not just bones that can become fossilized. Feathers and plants can, too!

## Frizzle Fact

Birds have hollow bones filled with air to make them lighter. Some dinosaur bones were like this, too.

## Tree creature

Early birds were about 20 inches (50 centimeters) long, which is about the same size as a goose.

It's possible that the first birds were dinosaurs that lived in trees. Flight evolved when they jumped from branch to branch, trying to escape from predators.

**Feathered friends!**

### What are feathers for?
by Wanda

Some experts think that many two-legged dinosaurs had feathers. Feathers are made from the same kind of material that's found in the scaly skin of a reptile and human hair and nails. Early feathers would have been branch-like scales growing out of the skin. These might have been for show, or they could have helped an animal keep warm.

Long feathers on the arms and legs might have been used to wrap around the body to help a dinosaur hide.

# Weird Dinos

S ome ancient reptiles looked nothing like animals that live on Earth today. For example, the Therizinosaurus stood 16 feet 6 inches (5 meters) tall on its back legs and had claws nearly 3 feet 6 inches (1 meter) long — the longest of any animal in history.

**Gigantspinosaurus was protected by two rows of bony plates along its back and one enormous spike behind each shoulder blade.**

**Therizinosaurus was a plant-eater. It might have used its long claws to pull down tall, springy branches to take a bite.**

**Therizinosauru probably used its claws to scare off predators.**

### Frizzle Fact

**Deinonychus had a hooked claw on its inner toe. It could flick this toe up and down, perhaps to slash at prey.**

Fossils reveal that Gigantoraptor was more than 12 feet (3.5 meters) tall. Scientists believe it had feathers on its arms, which it waved to frighten off attackers.

They're everywhere!

## Where did dinosaurs live?
by Arnold

When dinosaurs first appeared, it is likely that Earth's continents were all joined together. The land separated over millions of years. By the Cretaceous period, different types of dinosaurs had spread all over the world.

Triassic World Map (250–200 mya)

# Mass Extinction

**S**cientists believe that an asteroid crashed into Earth some 66 mya. The explosion created a cloud of dust that surrounded the planet for many years. Many plants couldn't grow in the cold and dark, so the dinosaurs began dying. On board the bus, we noticed the sky was growing dark now, too. "We'd better leave before *we* become extinct!" said the Friz.

Scientists say the asteroid that hit Earth was 6 miles (9.5 kilometers) wide. It landed in what is now Mexico's Yucatán Peninsula. At the time, the impact made a crater 124 miles (200 kilometers) wide — big enough to fit all of Los Angeles.

The exploding asteroid made a massive fireball. The impact was as powerful as a million of the biggest bombs humans can make.

End of an era!

## What is a mass extinction?
by Keesha

The dying out of the dinosaurs is called a mass extinction. Three-quarters of all the animals and plants on Earth were wiped out. Scientists know that there were four other mass extinctions before this one, because fossils of certain species seen in old rocks suddenly fail to appear in newer ones. But nobody really knows how these mass extinctions occurred.

### Frizzle Fact
The biggest mass extinction happened 252 mya. Just five percent of all animals that lived in the ocean survived.

# Amazing Dinosaurs

### Argentinosaurus

This dinosaur is named after the South American country in which its fossils were found. It lived around 95 mya. A giant plant-eater, it was one of the largest land-living dinosaurs. It was about 110 feet (33.5 meters) long, weighed almost 80 tons (75 tonnes), and had a long tail.

### Giganotosaurus

One of the biggest meat-eating dinosaurs ever found, Giganotosaurus was 25 feet (7.5 meters) tall and 50 feet (15 meters) long. It lived in South America about 100 mya. Its teeth were 8 inches (20 centimeters) long — as long as an adult's foot. Giganotosaurus cannot have been very smart. Its brain was the size of a banana!

### Iguanodon

This dinosaur was one of the first to be discovered. Its fossils were unearthed in England in 1809. Iguanodon lived around 130 mya. It was a plant-eater that walked on two legs. It had a long spiked claw on its thumb, possibly used for combat and self-defense.

### Microraptor

This little dinosaur lived in China around 125 mya. It was 3 feet (90 centimeters) long, and all four of its legs had long feathers like those on the wings of a bird. Scientists think that Microraptor could glide between the trunks of tall trees to escape predators and find small lizards and mouse-like mammals to eat.

## Pentaceratops

This huge plant-eating dinosaur lived around 70 mya. It had an enormous bony frill and five horns on its head. One surviving skull fossil is more than 10 feet (3 meters) long—as big as a car. It's the largest skull ever found of an animal that lived on land.

## Coelophysis

This fast-running reptile lived around 220 mya and was one of the earliest dinosaurs. It had a long, flexible neck and a mouth filled with sharp teeth. A very large collection of Coelophysis fossils—more than 1,000 skeletons—was discovered in New Mexico 70 years ago.

## Troodon

This two-legged dinosaur lived about 77 mya. It was 7 feet (2 meters) tall, fast-running, and had large eyes and a big brain (for a dinosaur). It also had hands that were good for holding objects and teeth that could bite through plant and animal foods. Troodon could survive in most habitats.

## Brachiosaurus

This dinosaur lived 150 mya and might be the tallest animal that ever lived. It had a neck that could have reached 35 feet (10 meters) into the sky—if its heart had been strong enough to pump blood all that way. Instead, Brachiosaurus's head stayed close to the ground.

Well done, class! Let's get ready for our next adventure!

# Fossil Hunting

**E**verything we know about dinosaurs comes from fossils dug up around the world. Experts on fossils are called paleontologists. These scientists use all the information they find about fossils to create an idea of how dinosaurs used to live.

A paleontologist carefully digs up some fossilized dinosaur eggs from a nest.

### ❮ Paleontologist

When a paleontologist finds a fossil, he or she first looks at the surrounding rocks for clues as to where the dinosaur died — perhaps in a desert or on a riverbed — and how old it is. Next, he or she removes all the fossil body parts from the rock. The shapes and sizes of the bones and teeth give the paleontologist an idea of the type of dinosaur and whether it was an adult or a baby at the time of death.

### ⌃ Computer Scientist

Fossil skeletons have no muscles or skin, so dinosaur experts use computers to work out how the animal might have moved when it was alive. They have programs that can connect the bones together — as well as add any bones that are missing from the fossil. Then they try to figure out where the muscles attached to the skeleton, and program this information into the computer model, too. The computer can then animate the skeleton, showing what the dinosaur could do — for example, how fast it could run and whether it stood up on its back legs or could swim in water.

### ❯ Paleobotanist

The rocks around dinosaur fossils sometimes contain tiny pieces of fossilized plants and other materials like bacteria. The remains of the dinosaur's last meal might also be found as part of a fossil. Experts called paleobotanists study fossilized plants and bacteria to figure out what the habitat was like when the dinosaur was alive. If the plants grew in water, for example, or were found on the side

of a mountain, scientists can get an idea as to how the animal adapted to living there and what its body would have been like.

# Words to Know

**Asteroid** A large rock that orbits the Sun. Asteroids are much smaller than planets.

**Continent** One of the seven large landmasses of Earth: Asia, Africa, Europe, North America, South America, Australia, and Antarctica.

**Crater** A large hole in the ground caused by something falling or exploding, such as an asteroid or a bomb.

**Dinosaur** A kind of large reptile that lived in prehistoric times.

**Evolve** To change slowly and naturally over time: Dogs and wolves evolved from one common ancestor.

**Extinct** A species that no longer exists. It is known about only through fossils.

**Fern** A plant that has feathery leaves, or fronds, and no flowers. Ferns usually grow in damp places and reproduce by spores instead of seeds.

**Fossil** A bone, shell, or other trace of an animal or plant from millions of years ago, preserved as rock.

**Habitat** The place that an animal usually lives.

**mya** A shorter way of writing "million years ago" when talking about the time dinosaurs lived on Earth.

**Predator** An animal that lives by hunting other animals for food.

**Prey** An animal that is hunted by another animal for food.

**Reptile** A cold-blooded animal with four legs, and a long tail.

**Rival** Two or more animals competing against each other.

**Sauropod** One of a group of large plant-eating dinosaurs with small heads and long necks and tails. An Apatosaurus is a sauropod.